Manic Deflecti   ;

50 More Life Poems

John Welsh

chipmunkapublishing
the mental health publisher

John Welsh

Published by
Chipmunkapublishing
PO Box 6872
Brentwood
Essex CM13 1ZT
United Kingdom

http://www.chipmunkapublishing.com

Copyright © John Welsh 2011

Edited by Aleks Lech

Chipmunkapublishing gratefully acknowledge the support of Arts Council England.

Introduction

"AS I LIVE MY LIFE IN VERSE"

This line from one of my poems does not mean I spend my days rhyming the events that happen to me; rather that often the triggers I see, hear and experience are stored and then come out later, sometimes much later, as a poetry title, then a poem.

This, my second book of verse, shows my early writing style from the 70's and the new found confidence I have gained to allow me to be more creative in the last few years since becoming a published author appeared on my c.v.

As with "Manic Reflections 50 life poems" this compilation of 50 more follows a strict order, i.e. alphabetical, and I am beginning to realise that as well as the poems, the stories behind them may eventually become source material for another book or a limited edition version.

My poetry is best, I feel, read out loud to intimate audiences and so for the last few years I have been developing my stage act. Like the writing bug, the performing bug has bitten me, and the pleasure at hearing generated laughter, gasps and applause is truly great.

I continue to manage my bipolar condition well and encourage all to write, paint or weave/sculpt etc. as a true therapy.

Author Biography

John Welsh lives in Lincoln but his origins are in his beloved Yorkshire. He is 57 and his life changed dramatically at 55 when he came out as a bipolar poet. He works in the sports and leisure industry. He has many passions in life including passion, nature, laughing and tennis but it is the creative writing and performing of it also framing up his personal poetry, then handing them to the customers that really floats his boat. He continues with his long term involvement with the University of Nottingham mental health nursing school doing regular presentations about living with bipolar disorder.

John Welsh

Thanks To

Old and new friends who say all the right words at the right time but like my family mainly let me get on with it and run a new verse or two past them now and again.

To my health advisers who on reading back seem to have been a source of regular triggers in this second book.

To all the girls I know who have a strong pulse (YOU KNOW WHO YOU ARE)

I love you now and tomorrow.

John Welsh

A BIG BONNY BIRD

Bum like a bus
Thighs like two drums
Arms like a wrestler
Dimples like plums

Chins resting on bosoms
Bosoms resting on belly
Has not seen her feet since??
Does not switch off the telly

But for all this I am not put off
She is certainly well fed
And we go up together
To our reinforced bed

John Welsh

A MAN'S GOTTA DO

No fixed destination
I've got no plan or guide
I'm walking blind through this wide world
I don't know what I'll find
I never do get serious
I treat the women cool
I say that I may stick around
But I am only passing through
The highways are my arteries
The byways are my veins
My heart lies in an unfound place
That's why I cannot remain

AFRICAN SUSAN

I decided to go walkabout
Afar with wide intent
New views, new lands, new people
On the African continent
But embarking on my research
With journal, atlas and net
I knew I would only gain the knowledge
From someone I had met
A meeting was made formal
And ideas they were born
So it was off with plans and biscuits
To the village of Hackthorn
Wall maps in the chapel
Artefacts at which I could gape
The target area narrowed
From the jungle to the Cape
Sue and I got cosy
A chat and cup of tea
Africa vast and exciting
She sold it thrice to me
Time passed oh so quickly
And this I can truly tell
These are places I've not been to
And most I cannot spell
Sue painted a picture
On the canvas of my mind
Mountains, rivers larger than life
All these there I would find

John Welsh

So my appetite is wetted
For this new continental ride
Oh just one more question
Will you be my tour guide?

ARE YOU LISTENING?

So you are not in the speech
No you are not mentioned
Because you hijack the talk
I have seen your intention

So I avoid your presence
Cross the road and hide
I know what the outcome
Will be on your side

Am I becoming you?
Do I look just one way?
Let me know what you think
Tell me what I'll say

Now all conversations ended
All debate has gone to bed
Maybe night will forget morning
And all that was said

Try to hear and not be heard
Try to speak when lines are fed
Respect the souls around you
Or they will hope that you are dead

John Welsh

BEYONCE SPOOF

If I was a boy
I would drink beer then some wine
I'd drink beer in the morning
In fact I'd drink beer all the time

I would be sick in my shoes
Wake up with girls I don't know
And when I looked at them closely
I'd just want to get up and go

Have an intravenous drip
To keep my beer levels high
And hope I am never sober
Not even on the day that I die

So here's a toast to us men
Let the party begin
I'm going off beer and wine
Now where is the vodka and gin?

CHERRY SWEET, CHERRY TART

Born on a full moon
Convent trained
Skin like a gypsy
Eyes unrestrained
Became an earth goddess
Ran, laughed and teased
The boys queued and jostled
Then fell to her knees
I met her at hay time
I was having a nap
The day hour was sultry
And high was the sap
She opened with "You're new"
She was silhouetted by the sun
"Yes I am working a passage"
My ticket had come!
She said "Would you like me to
Show you a place?"
We strolled off together
It turned into a race
Her laughter was bell like
Her feet dusty and bare
The incline of her head showed
The promise was there
The deep cool pool inviting
A shyness not there
I felt a slight foreboding
As if entering a lair

John Welsh

Dry she was a temptress
Wet she was a dream
Her lips full and hungry
She pushed my extreme
She left me on bankside
Got up, slipped away
Her heat, her tongue, her eyes
Stay with me to this day

DIAMOND DAY

Now Joan and Jack are quite a pair
Members of groups and sport
Regulars around the village
Involved in skills and how they're taught

From growing, bowling, W.I. and church
They spread their interests wide
So is it an in or out night?
It's very hard to decide

Jack was in the baccy trade
Joan served meals on trays
He said I only smoked after meals
And got down to 40 meals a day

Joan looked up from her bowling stance
Her eye saw a way through
She said that's the jack
I want to get closer to

As like a garden they have grown together
Like bowls they came to touch
Their diamond day is special
60 years means so much.

Have a great day
John

John Welsh

FIVE MINUTES OF HONESTY

Sit down with a stranger
Talk, smile, choose and pick
Know them through their responses
On any given topic

Trust them with your skeletons
Your demons, your illness and cares
Know truth is locked between you
Which no one else will share

Five minutes of honesty
Is worth a lifetime's blank face
It's the compassion and the listening
The friendship and the space

When I go I want you near me
And if my thoughts I cannot tell
You can interpret my fading eyes
And laugh for me as well

I never was a rich man
With coin, or gold, or art
But my wealth is so extensive
As I live in people's hearts

Looking back at bedtime
On the day that was my life
Those moments shared, those moments cared
When peace and joy ran rife

FOLLOW THE COUNTRYSIDE CODE

Watch out for the townies
Especially in cars
They do not understand narrow
And ask endless questions in bars

They will park on a corner
Let their dogs out to run
And when the weather turns lousy
Well they do not have much fun

But I as a Yorkshire landlord
Forgive them all their ills
As long as they remember
To put their money in my tills

John Welsh

GRIEF

My today's seem like tomorrows
As I work my short term plan
I miss the bus, get soaking wet
My world has overran

Whereas the seconds were ticking
It now seems it's the hours
I buy fresh cut stems from the florist
But the vase takes only dead flowers

A light went out in the world
But what to show or say
I loved him then as I love him now
I cry until empty

HEALTH+WEALTH =HAPPINESS

The measures of a lifetime
Are clearly there to tell
The one that's most important
Is the state of being well

Next up there is solvency
No debt, no stress, no woes
Being able to live your life
As far as your wealth goes

With these in place what follows
A better time is had
To enjoy your days freely
Happy not often sad

John Welsh

HELP ME NO

A feeling of panic
A shortage of breath
There is an ache in my stomach
Could this mean my death?

My head thoughts are spinning
Indecision and doubt
Should I go to the doctors?
What is this all about?

I tried to ignore it
Gave reason a shove
But it seems the diagnosis
Is I am probably in love.

I SAW NOTHING

These new boots are the business
I wear them every day
I watch them as I walk along
Avoiding mud and spray

My new phone is the latest
Photos, videos, net and calls
I use it on the pavement
One eye looks out for trip falls

The I pod I am playing
Takes me to a higher place
So if I meet you in the street
Then out will be my face

Is there hope for conversation
Face to face with time to spare
Or do I have to text you
To see if you are there?

John Welsh

IF I LOST MY SENSES

If I lost my touch
Of the feel of living fur
And the textured life I lead

If I lost my smell of
That ocean side salt fresh breeze
And that early bacon frying call to table

If I lost my hearing of
Those church bells calling and
The wind rising in the trees

If I lost my sight
I would cry through unseeing eyes
And all my views would become memories

If I lost my senses I would lose my life

IN A GODDESS'S CHARMS

She seemed just like a goddess
So I used my rule of thumb
And watched when she bent over
To see the sun shine out of her bum

She noticed my attention
So I tried to pass it off
But I was on a loser
Out came an embarrassed cough

She questioned my proximity
I said that I was lost
The goddess went into reject mode
On my arse I was tossed

I decided to cut my losses
Bottle it and leave town
There was no extra illumination
I checked while I was down

So goddesses I give wide berths to
It seems a safer bet
I am moving on to princesses
A pea I need to get

John Welsh

IT SUITS ME

Speeding along in a Lotus Elan
Cash in my pocket, not having much fun
Dreaming about all the things still not done
I like my bike, it suits me

Impatiently waiting in a Vauxhall Corsair
Ten miles from Skeggy and no road to spare
Time to return just as soon as we're there
I like my bike, it suits me

Cruising along in my Rolls Silver Cloud
Move over small fry see you don't crowd
This is the real thing, that's why I am so proud
I still like my bike, it suits me

ITCHY CROTCH

Now that spring is coming
And sap rises in the plants
I have started to remember
What happens in my pants

I often use a coat hanger
A screwdriver or a spoon
But I need a longer finger
To reach that inner moon

It comes to me in public
After walk, run or race
That unbearable irritant
Is mirrored in my face

I will suffer it till Autumn
With respite in the shower
That sodding itch like a manic bitch
Who nags me hour by hour

John Welsh

IT'S ONLY NATURAL

Nature gives us texture and form
Contrast and movement, variety and hue
With trees heading for the sun
And shrubs that stay low
Leave them unattended
And see where they grow

The flowers burst forth and
Stay whilst they can
For bees to rub legs on
Or picked for the tables of man

Is there a price on that beauty?
Why not enjoy and go past?
Let it bloom, seed and wilt there
And the cycle will last

LITS GIT WIT IN GODZONE

The road trip plan was easy
this is what we'd seek
places beginning with P and R
and W's next week

The van room it was spacious
lockers for all our crap
bang your head! stub your toe!
try to get a nap

The straight/windy road is calling
memories there to keep
I often woke up knackered
I'd been driving in my sleep

North and South we ventured
cities ,hills and bays
lost count of the mileage
the regions and the days

All Godzone things around us
are sent from heaven above
but if you cannot get a view
give the crowd a shove

We ate our way cross country
local fruit, fish and ham
but the tables were overturned
when a parrot bit our van

John Welsh

The waters kept us going
ocean, sea and thermal spa
the lakes, rivers and waterfalls
and the beer in the bar

We stopped counting livestock
cattle, sheep and goat
vicuna, deer and elephant!
the bison got my vote

Out on the blue and bumpy
chasing sperm and dolphin fin
but what's this handed to me?
a bag to put my muesli in

The cricket sounds in the bush
seem to signify heat
the main tourist attractions
seem to signify feet

Not all is good in Paradise
with sand flies who like to bite
and just when its time to settle
there's a possum up your pipe

My favourite sister Morticia
tried to organise my day
from my bowels to my shopping
she had to have her say

Manic Deflections

What to leave out in this poem
is difficult intention
LOTR, crayfish, guinness
all deserve a mention

Ellen says it's warts and all
I say bruises and bites
there are 5 hours in the camcorder
and I hold the movie rights

(The other 46 verses are with the immigration
control people. this will not make much sense to
anyone who has not been to NZ, spent time in a
camper van with a mad woman who likes the
backwaters, or just enjoys going HURRAH AND
LASHINGS OF GINGER BEER)

John Welsh

A LONG WAY FROM AOTEAROA

If I had a thousand pounds
To spend upon a dream
Then I think I would invest it
On a journey once extreme

A return to New Zealand
And this is what I'd like
Instead of going camper van
I'd tour it on a bike

Two panniers and a sister
Is all that I would need
I would collect the roadkill daily
The barbecue to feed

With my Ellen pedalling strongly
I could enjoy the view
It's a tandem life for her
I would prepare the stew

Camp out every evening
Pitch the tent and how
Make sure the sodding sand flies
Are biting sheep and cow

Would visit Coromandel,
Bay of Islands, Eastern shore
See the quiet, untrod places
The lanes that lead to more

On my list is Invercargill

Manic Deflections

That southern island tip
Take a ferry over to Stewart
Would likely have a nip

One year on I remember
Those vales, those peaks, those shores
So keep a welcome in New Zealand
I am knocking on your door

John Welsh

MANIC DEFLECTIONS

Frustrate and delay me
Say no, don't tell me why
Leave it hanging in limbo
Like small blue in a clouded sky

Is there chance of a decision
So that I can then move on
Or will time decide the outcome
One day = day one

Maybe it's my condition
Maybe it's my pace
Can it be my dogged stare
The urgency in my face

I should know by now
My hand in a fire will be burnt
But I will continue and continue
The truth grail is all I want

MISSING THE PRINT

How to interpret
The thoughts between the lines
Those almost near reflections
Of close remembered times

Only you know the story
From mind unto the page
Only you know plot and ending
The secret of the sage

When souls are bared and shared
With open intimacy
Then thanks for a window
Into your privacy

Dedications to My Children

NIC NIC

NIC YOU ARE ON YOUR WAY
WITH BOTH FEET ON THE FLOOR
THE ONLY WAY IS FORWARD NOW
TRUE JOY IS THROUGH THAT DOOR
ALL MY LOVE DAD

MY JO

Jo you've had your birthday poem
So this is a short review
I feed off your ideas and energy
As I live my life near you
ALL MY LOVE DAD

MY SON MIKE

MIKE YOU ARE A CRAZY HORSE
YOUR LEGS JUST RUN AND RUN
NEVER STOP AND NEVER CHANGE
YOU ARE MY FAVOURITE SON
ALL MY LOVE DAD

NO MATRON NOOOOOOO

She comes to me at night
Increases my medication
Loosens two top buttons
And lets me sleep alone
She soothes my inner turmoil
Lubricates my need and straining
Takes control when I am helpless
She gives this dog a bone

And for this I think I am grateful
Her uniform and demeanour
The hard truth and my changing
Taught me to be sane
So release me from this jacket
Let me run barefoot in Eden
And howl tonight at moonlight
And administer my wolf's bane

John Welsh

NON PARTICIPATION = NON APPRECIATION

The morning woke and shone, it was a special day
The children knew the treats in store, the parents
knew they would pay
It's Juliana's birthday and it heralds summer's start
And all the people of that city will in some way take
part

The stallholders are busy laying out their wares
But there is a hush in the streets as if no one
seems to dare
To start the celebrations early
For the day is long and promises many things
It's Juliana's birthday, think of the pleasure it will
bring

The flags were raised last evening to remind those
who forgot
And strangers like me will say that's good, why not
For she is very popular and her people really care
I am glad today is sunny, I am glad that I am here

(Amsterdam 1977)

Sequel follows later in the book

NURSE I AM GOING IN

I paid my N.I. contributions
And now and then for scripts
But lately it's been payback time
As my body creaked and ripped

I have an impressive belly scar
That I show off at the pool
The grandson says it's where an alien came out
When he is out of school

So I have been called back in a second time
For anaesthetic and drugged kip
If this pattern continues
I will insist they fit a zip

John Welsh

OH DEARY WEARY ME

On rising from my slumbers
With the toilet as my aim
I entwined myself in bedding
And fell to the floor in pain

I tripped on pants and t-shirt
Left from last day's wear
The wardrobe is no more
It's good I keep a spare

In my haste to leave the bedroom
The door being not ajar
My judgement of the exit
Meant I didn't go too far

So with quilt still wound around me
And with door print on my face
And bladder alarm still sounding
What I needed was some pace

At last the bathroom handle
I entered with a slip
As I lay in pain and urine
The flow and then the drip

ONLY A POET

Some say complex
I say confused
The day's uncertain
With clarity underused

I only want a simple life
A knowing nod and smile
Often speech was surplus
No side, no edge, no guile

But it was all a dream state
And truth often became a curse
But the explanation is clearer now
As I live my life in verse

ONLY THE LONELY

Look for a soul mate
Search out a friend
Know in an instant
Truth will not bend

Share out the challenge
Hearts bold as one
Laugh and congratulate
As victory is won

Stay in the quiet times
Share sadness and joy
Know them, their feelings
Be it girl or a boy

Hearts and souls are for sharing
So look for that bond
Share all your life blood
With one blue eyed blonde

PARANOID HYPOCHONDRIA WITH MAN FLU SYMPTOMS

I DO NOT FEEL QUITE MYSELF TODAY
A LETHARGY, A WEIGHT
AS IF ALL MY BORES ARE NOT ON FULL
CHARGE
AND MY BODY IS OFF STRAIGHT

ON INSPECTION IN THE MIRROR
OF TONGUE, OF EYE, OF SKIN
IT ONLY NEEDS THE AUTOPSY
OF THE KIND OF STATE I AM IN

SO IS IT FIRST AID KIT, CHEMIST OR GP
THAT'S NEEDED TO SAVE ME
OR MAYBE THE START OF SYMPTOMS
THAT WILL SEND ME TO A AND E

THERE IS SOMETHING TO BE SAID FOR
NATURAL
ALTERNATE REMEDIES RECEIVE SOME
PRAISE
ONE WAS IMMERSE IN WARM COW DUNG
AND LEAVE FOR THREE WHOLE DAYS

I AM JUST PAST A WINTER ILLNESS
BRONCHIAL COUGH , WET NOSE AND CHILL
I TRIED A HONEY DEW MELON UP MY ARSE
AND CALLED IT A SLOW RELEASE PILL

PERFUME AND CLEAVAGE

So I'm getting dolled up
For a bit of a do
It will be a long evening
So take comfort in shoe

We will be chatting and eating
Drinking wine, candles lit
Then flinging the knees up
To the sound of the hits

There will be perfume and cleavage
DJ's and bows
As the band strikes the 1st note
Up will go the tempo

All the highlights and teeth shine
In the frenetic pace
The ball lets its hair down
Over its bright shiny face

The last waltz is coming
So ladies and gents please
Let's end this great evening
With a smile, dance and squeeze

PLANK STACKER'S LAMENT

I think that I will never see
A picture lovely as a tree
But I will refuse and say no thanks
At even looking at any more planks

For five weeks now I have planked away
And what have I to show
Ten blistered fingers and splintered clothes
And a fair amount of dough

With the noise of the saw cutting deep through my
brain
I am keeping my eye on the overhead crane
And I am trying my hardest to keep fairly sane
But an existence like this is against my grain

The factory is modern
With the air made pure and clear
But every time I cough now
I get a planking souvenir

I dream of things I'd buy if rich
I dream of wildest loves
I dream of what I really need
A brand new pair of planking gloves

Often in the night I'd wake
And lonely vigil keep
The secrets which I now reveal
I'd been planking in my sleep

REASONS I CAN'T

She is fitting a cat flap
Washing her hair
Expecting a man
To do a boiler repair

There's a repeat on the telly
That she's missed before
Her VCR's broken
Her hard drive's no more

Her friend needs a shoulder
She is coming with wine
Her wardrobe is empty
It's all on the line

You pick up a signal
And so ask her out
And then start to wonder
What it's all about

I don't think I will bother
Following it through
As I am busy right now
A short text will do

REQUITED REFLECTIONS

On evenings when the day's work is done
And the world is winding down
I'd often think of times we had
The shared joys we have known

Around the lazy cosy hours
I'd wake and be aware
Of summer days and foolish ways
When we didn't have a care

On waking from my dream bed
Sleep lingering in my brain
I'd try to piece together
The memories that remain

And even in my day peak
When the world is dash and pace
The madness and the panic
Will mirror your calm face

John Welsh

RESPONSES FROM A SLEEPLESS NIGHT

A quiet time, a voice called out
Not wail or cry or moan or shout
But a nation dying on its knees
A barren plain where once grew trees

I've watched it grow from stammering birth
And rise to high esteem
I saw the mortal thrust strike home
The speculator's dream

Its sense of purpose, strength and age
The essential part of whole
Neglect, decay and apathy
Destroyed its inner soul

The undermining that followed
Allowed protests not to set
And then they condemned the site
By offering " to let"

The rates were high
The rents were mad
And plumbing near extinct
The squat was not what it was supposed to be
We tiddled in the sink

RESTLESS URGE

I feel a poem coming on
But know not when or how
A throbbing juicy loving ride
And all words rhyme with now

Tbc

This is the reader participation part. You continue it!

John Welsh

RIGHT UP MY NOSE

Today I saw a field of rape seed
Blossom in the sun
Soon when pollen spores start to rise
My breathing days will be gone

The colour yellow is my friend
It cheers and warms and glows
But this plant is the only crop
That irritates my nose

The ridge view is impressive
Trent vale a patchwork frieze
But it is never in clear focus
My eyes stream and then I sneeze

Four weeks on it's fading
Bees came as swarming mists
Whilst I was buying tablets
At the local chemists

RON SEAL

We all like Ron
He really is a trooper
Always up for a chat
Even when his face is in a bowl of souper

With most of his own teeth
And some of his hair
Mention a game of tennis
And he will be there

He is a hit with the ladies
A ready smile on his lips
I am not sure how he does it
But I am picking up tips

He is a demon on court
Teaching others as well
Sharing his craft
You should hear him YELL

With his thick Arran jumper
And newspaper under arm
It's amazing he can serve
Over arm

He lives on a boat you know
A moored cruiser, no tub
Mind you he doesn't always get home
Twice he has been locked in the club

Happy Birthday Ron, you do exactly what it says on the tin

SCALLYWAG OR SAINT

I tried to be a good boy
Every day of my long life
Reliable and dependable
So I could win a wife

I told the honest truth mostly
Even when it hurt
But bit my tongue on Fridays
To raise my chance of skirt

So ask me my opinion
Discuss an open view
When two minds meet and blend
Could it be me and you?

Please be there beside me
When chaos turns to woe
Transfix me with your innocence
Let your feelings show

All I want is timeless
A hug, a kiss, a bond
Could you be the one to deliver
This eternal feeling fond?

If it's no then I'll recover
Time will heal and blur
The hopes, the dreams, the outcome
Love lies bleeding at my door.

John Welsh

SEQUEL TO JULIANA'S BIRTHDAY

It's Juliana's birthday
And the brollies have come out
And all the folk
Will laugh and shout
As the hailstones hit their face
It's Juliana's birthday
Cheers! To you your grace

I may go out this evening
I might just walk a mile
I'll look in the shop windows
And I will probably smile
And think it's great to be alive

THE GATES ARE PADLOCKED

St Peter can you tell me
When I called yester eve
There was no reply, the lights were out
I shouted but no answer received

I had come up specially
On a quiet day I thought
To miss that holiday traffic
And the carnage that it brought

So where are all the angels
The honest decent no mores
The saint like and the good folk
Who reside behind heaven's door?

Away on their jollies
Out to lunch and late
Must be out for quite some time
So secure that pearly gate

I hung around for ages
There was no one there to tell
Made my mind up in an instant
My new address is HELL

John Welsh

THE ONE

The keep me hanging on
That touch, not much
Those eyes, are there lies
The chance meet
Those in step feet
The leaving and the greeting
The time spent, words meant
So where are your feelings
Above, below and wide
So take a chance
Engage and dance
The future will decide

THE POWER AND THE SWERVE

To exercise and socialise
Is one of life's shared bliss
I found my perfect sport early
I call the game tennis

The racquet seemed to be
An extension of my arm
I even play out in winter
I soon get warm

40 years onwards
The joys are still the same
Sociable yet serious
I love this ball game

John Welsh

THE TAMING OF MY THOUGHTS

I used care as a watchword
I tried to not upset
I'd pause as if unsure
Dip a toe but not get wet

Think it, do not speak it
Store it in your mind
Say only platitudes
Try to be kind

It's changed now I'm older
Though I still give a damn
Outspoken and outrageous
A too honest man

Gut instincts have taught me
To find the friends I love
Laughter and joy have brought me
To heavens above

THE WALLS ARE QUIET

High ramparts, sentinel tower
Open drawbridge invites the tour
Union flag, defiant roar
It was not once come the hour

For what reason
Was it Church or King
Did battle start then
Sword and axe did swing

Those that fell were soldiers
Husbands, brothers and son
Each a story to relate
They died as many and as one

Cobbles cover bloodstains
Cameras record a later scene
But listen very carefully
Hear the shouts and panic screams

History is written
It is re-enacted, filmed and shown
Very hard to believe now
This happened in this town

John Welsh

THE WASHING OF MY FACE

Another day
Another way
To stem the flow
And how to show
A face that's brave
Not rant or rave
Serene and calm
But where's the harm
In breaking up
Emotion's full cup
Sadness and joy
In girl or boy
So let the tears flow
Sob, let them go
It's a natural peace
Washing soul and face

THESE ARE MY DREAMS

To ride a white stallion through mist shrouded
marshes on a crisp Autumn morning with the sun a
pale yellow
To dive in a green pool and fathom its secrets, the
life that abounds there washed with shadows and
sun rays
To dance on a beach with the wine coursing
through me and shout out to Bacchus whose
madness is on me
To sing to a princess with a face like an infant, her
eyes bright with wonder as they change with the
tempo
To wake in the night and listen to the breathing of a
loved one who is cooking my breakfast that
morning
To sit on a mountain and drink in the riches of a
landscape so wondrous and a country so vast

John Welsh

WHOM THEY MAY CONCERN

To win <u>they</u> said was right
To lose <u>they</u> said no shame
I tried them both and found no peace
It is <u>they</u> who are to blame

<u>They</u> say it isn't good
To hurry through your food
Ha! <u>They</u> must have had indigestion
To make this bold reflection

I'd heard of <u>them</u> so looked around
To question <u>them</u> in depth
But no one could advise me
Of a path <u>they</u> may have kept

I often thought of <u>them</u>
and what <u>they</u> would have done
but now its only <u>I</u>
and <u>I</u> seem not so alone

TWO BLONDES AND A CORKSCREW

The evening started happily
Vodka with our tea
Sod the food, we were rude
My best mate and me

Snogged some bloke in Silver St
Though I have a cold
Can't remember much about him
Was he young or old?

Showed our bras at half past 9
Flashed them good and flashed them quick
Laughed and cried like two mad birds
Made us both be sick

Got a caution from the plod
Said we were out of order
It's frowned upon to urinate
On the flower border

My mouth is like a parrot's cage
My face and hair a sight
Just time to do some maintenance
Before the planned hen night

John Welsh

WORDS I CANNOT SAY

In every life there is a time
When love and hate begin to rhyme
As chaos rules each clock chime
Ignites the yearning, so I mime

Think it don't deliver them
Bite the tongue, anger stem
Calm, deep breaths, become solemn
Wait for peace, hum Jerusalem

Hope you know the time is right
Choose it well not past midnight
Words can start or end the fight
Silences may not or might

Lightning Source UK Ltd.
Milton Keynes UK
24 February 2011

168174UK00001B/18/P